That First Kiss
and Other Stories

That First Kiss and Other Stories

Lisa Calderone-Stewart
Ed Kunzman

Saint Mary's Press
Christian Brothers Publications
Winona, Minnesota

We dedicate this book to the next generation:

Emily Jean Banset
Rebecca Ann Banset
Thomas Joseph Banset
Nicholas Robert Bidroski
Scott Jeffrey Bidroski
Andrea Elaine Bottger
Kristin Marie Bottger
Sean Norman Bottger
Barbara Ann Calderone
Bernadette Rose Calderone
Elizabeth Constance Calderone
Elizabeth Katherine Grubb
Sarah Irene Grubb
Eric Michael Hagan
Kelly Suzanne Hagan
Mary Elizabeth Hagan
Christine Michelle Hladik
Gregory Stewart Hladik
Jennifer Susan Hladik
Robert Joseph Hladik
Adam Franklin Jacobs
Billie Lee Kunzman

Paige Denise Kunzman
Rahne Lane Kunzman
Ri Albert Kunzman
Conor Patrick McGhehey
Jill Renee McGhehey
Molly Maureen McGhehey
Tate David McGhehey
Casey (KC) John Moscrip
Hilary Ann Moscrip
Jared Paul Moscrip
Brian James Stewart
Jill Elizabeth Stewart
Kelsey Lynn Stewart
Kerry Jean Stewart
Michael James Stewart
Ralph Pierre Stewart
Brianna Lynn Thompson
David Edward Towey
Elizabeth Susan Towey
Aaron Thomas Willey
Gretchen Michelle Willey
Richard Paul Willey

The precious gift of faith that we were given we now happily hand on to you—in fulfillment of Jesus' desire: "The gift you have received, give as a gift" (Matthew 10:8).

Genuine recycled paper with 10% post-consumer waste.
Printed with soy-based ink.

The publishing team included Brian Singer-Towns, develop-
ment editor; Cheryl Drivdahl, copy editor; Alan S. Hanson, pro-
duction editor and typesetter; Stephan Nagel, cover designer;
PhotoDisc Inc., cover photo; pre-press, printing, and binding
by the graphics division of Saint Mary's Press.

The acknowledgments continue on page 92.

Printed in the United States of America.

Printing: 9 8 7 6 5 4 3 2 1

Year: 2007 06 05 04 03 02 01 00 99

ISBN 0-88489-589-0

Contents

Preface

Life is filled with opportunities for sharing stories. We share stories with classmates at school, with friends at parties, and with relatives at family gatherings. We read stories in books, watch stories on television and in movies, and write stories for English class. We even read stories in chat rooms on the Internet and swap stories by e-mail.

Whenever we listen to good stories, we find ourselves responding in a variety of ways: we laugh and we cry, we tremble in fear and we sigh in relief, we throw up our hands in disbelief and we nod in agreement. We respond in these ways because good stories are like mirrors: they give us a reflection of ourselves. The joys and sorrows of the stories' characters reflect our own joys and sorrows: we laugh and we cry from the heart because we recognize ourselves in the tales being told.

Some of the most meaningful stories that people share focus on growing up. These are stories of going to school and playing sports, of losing friends and finding new ones, of falling in love and breaking up. These are also stories that try to deal with the big questions of life: What kind of person do I want to be? Where is my life going? How do I relate to my family? What kinds of people do I want for friends? How do I make difficult decisions? What do I really believe in? Who is God?

This book is a collection of stories about young people. The characters in these stories experience wonder and struggle, hurt and forgiveness, failure and success, tears and laughter, learning and relearning. In other words, these stories are very much like your own. You are invited to use them as mirrors for looking at your own life.

After every story in this book, you will find a set of questions to help you take a deeper look at yourself. The title of this set of questions is "Seeing Your Own Story." When you think about the issues and events in your own life that the stories reflect back to you, you can begin to see yourself in a new light and learn more about the unique person you are.

After the reflection questions is a section called "Seeing the Faith Story." This section is designed to help you make connections between what you are discovering about yourself and what it means to be a believer in God, a Christian, and a Catholic. The questions at the end of this section can help you view your own life through the eyes of faith.

This book is one in a series of five. The other books in the series are entitled *My Wish*

List and Other Stories, Better than Natural and Other Stories, Straight from the Heart and Other Stories, and *Meeting Frankenstein and Other Stories.* Each book in the series presents several opportunities for you to discover more about your own story, to examine your own issues, and to search for your own answers about life, God, and faith.

It is our hope that once you see your deeper self through the mirrors of these stories, you will continue to reflect on the important matters of life. We believe that life becomes happier and more meaningful when we take the time to be reflective. A word of caution: Looking into the mirror of a story may become an exciting, lifelong habit!

That First Kiss

Pete's Journal   Thursday, 2 June

Yesterday was the worst day of my life—
ever! Why did I have to drop that tray of
plates when the restaurant was full of people? And then why did I have to slip in the
mess and split my pants when everyone was
looking at me? Can you believe my luck? My
boss told me that all busboys drop at least
one tray on the job, but why did I have to
do it in front of the most beautiful girl in the
world? I guess I just lost my cool when I noticed Alexis in the booth with her friends.
After trying for weeks to impress her, I ended up showing her my underwear!

»   »   »   «   «   «

Pete's Journal   Friday, 1 July

I can't believe that Alexis is in love with
me—Peter T. Norrington! Wow! My heart
races just thinking about her. Alexis is everything I've ever dreamt of—and more. When
I saw her at Ten Flags three weeks ago, and

she smiled at me, I couldn't believe my eyes. I almost jumped over the park fence when she gave me her phone number and told me to give her a call. Didn't she remember the night I nearly exposed my backside to her?

"She's too pretty," my best friend, Isaac, keeps telling me. "She's just playing with you, Pete. When she finds someone better, she'll drop you like a wild pitch!"

"How do you know, Isaac?" I always challenge him, faking a confident smile and telling myself that he's just jealous. "Maybe she's stuck on me for good."

"Someone's stuck, for sure," he says, "like a fly in a cobweb. And you're the fly, buddy, not Alexis."

If it were only Isaac's voice that fed my doubts, I wouldn't be so worried. But last week, Dad also warned me about pretty girls. "Girls like her want to call the shots, Pete," he said. "Remember: if something seems too good to be true, it probably is." And Mom's always reminding me that I'm too young to get serious about a relationship. "There are a lot of fish in the sea, Peter," she tells me whenever I mention Alexis's name. "Maybe you should keep your eyes open."

Well, my eyes have been open for years, and I've seen dozens of pretty fish in the big sea, but not one of them was ever interested in me. Why is it so terrible for me to fall in love with a beautiful girl who's also in love with me? I've never felt more alive in all my life! I can't wait to go through senior year with an honest-to-goodness girlfriend. It's about time for me to experience a little bit of the "good life" and not just talk about it!

When Uncle Frank gets home from his trip to Europe, I'm going to take Alexis over to meet him. Frank's always been a good friend, more like a brother to me than an uncle. He'll help me to understand why no one believes me right now. I'll show him the poem that Alexis gave me yesterday and dare him to side with those who think she doesn't really love me. "Like water on the lip of a red, red rose," she wrote, "you are life and refreshment to me." Frank will recognize true love when he sees it!

Yes, Frank will support me. When I was only nine years old, and he was a point guard on the local high school's basketball team, he used to come up to me after every game—win or lose—and carry me on his shoulders to the dressing room. He didn't have to give me all that attention, but he did. And even when the other guys teased him about his "runt of a friend," he didn't forget me after the next game. I think that's where I had my first taste of true friendship.

And isn't that exactly how Alexis is treating me now? She doesn't have to give me so much attention or spend so much time with me, but she does. And even though Isaac called her a praying mantis the other night before the baseball game, she ran over to the dugout to congratulate me after my first home run of the season—and simply smiled at Isaac, who was standing next to me. I was so excited I hit a double the next time at bat!

What else can I say—except that what's happening right now seems too good to be true? When Alexis gave me that first kiss on 22 June, I knew then it was the real thing. And nothing since then has changed my mind. That's why I asked her tonight to go with me to the homecoming dance in the fall—and she accepted!

Can you believe my luck? The guy who nearly fell on his face trying to impress the girl of his dreams ends up standing square on his feet! Today's the best day of my life— ever!

Seeing Your Own Story

- Are Pete's feelings for Alexis true love or simple infatuation, or perhaps a mixture of the two? Why do you think so? Is there any wisdom in Pete's parents' words of caution? If so, try to express it in your own words.
- In the Bible, there is a love song—believe it or not! It's called the Song of Solomon (or

the Song of Songs). For centuries, both Jews and Christians have interpreted the Song as a symbol of the love between God and the human race. What similarities do you see between the thrill of young love and the age-old love of God for us? What differences do you see?

Seeing the Faith Story

Christians call the message of Jesus Christ the Good News. This message is that God loves us unconditionally, even when we don't feel especially loved or lovable. Like Pete, we sometimes wonder how we can be so fortunate, particularly when our own pain, feelings of unworthiness, and the unbelief of others cause us to doubt. At times we may wonder, Is the Good News just too good to be true?

For this reason, we read and reread God's "love letters" in the Holy Bible (often called the Scriptures), and we listen over and over again to the wonderful stories and teachings handed down by generations of believers (usually called Tradition). As a community of faith with deep roots and high hopes, we support one another in our efforts to believe and to live as believers.

This book focuses on the important teachings of the Christian faith that are highlighted in an ancient prayer called the Apostles' Creed. By looking at the various statements of this prayer, we can find out what is distinctive and attractive about the Christian community of faith. Along the way, we may also discover—or rediscover—why those who identify themselves as followers of Jesus Christ have much to celebrate.

- Do you have any questions or concerns about the Christian faith in general or about the Catholic church in particular? If so, what are they? If you are a Catholic Christian, are you excited about your religious identity or do you rarely think about it? If you are not a Catholic Christian, is there anything about the Catholic church that appeals to you?

Let us profess our faith.

When You Care Enough to Give the Very Best

Consuela and Heather were best friends. They had both moved into the city last February, and had now known each other for exactly one year. Being new at their school together had bonded them in a special way. They shared everything—secrets, promises, future dreams, and disappointments. They even had the same birthday—17 February!

This year, they decided to get together on their birthday to exchange presents. Consuela was an only child, and both of her parents were finishing work at their offices that evening, so the two friends chose to meet at Consuela's house. Heather was relieved because at her house, her three younger brothers would have been running around, crazy with the excitement of having a visitor and impossible to control.

As she walked to her friend's, Heather hoped Consuela would like the present she had created. Heather's family could barely make ends meet, and her mother did some sewing at home to make extra money. One thing her family had a lot of was scrap fabric pieces and thread. So Heather had made a small quilt banner for Consuela, with one panel to represent each of the twelve months they had known each other. She had learned to quilt from her grandmother, as a child, and she thought this was her finest work yet.

When Heather arrived at her friend's, Consuela insisted that she open her gift first. It was a box wrapped in very heavy paper, with some kind of embossed logo. Heather opened the gift slowly, careful not to tear the paper. After separating the tissue inside the box, she held up a beautiful red velvet dress—the kind of fancy dress her mother had made for many other women, but had never had the money to make for herself or for Heather. Heather was speechless. Then she recognized the logo on the wrapping paper. It was the designer label from the company that had made the dress—which sold its clothing only at a very expensive store you needed an appointment to shop in.

"My turn!" said Consuela, before Heather even had the chance to thank her. She opened her gift quickly, ripping the paper to shreds as she struggled to get the lid off the box. "Oh, my!" she said as she examined every square of the quilt, remembering the event each panel symbolized.

The two of them sat on the couch in awkward silence for a moment. Consuela suggested that they eat some cookies or have some hot chocolate, but Heather didn't feel hungry. She kept fingering the thick, red velvet of her new dress, wondering how much it had cost. Probably more than her family's entire monthly budget. She became very quiet, trying to understand the feelings this new gift was bringing on.

Aware of her friend's discomfort, Consuela asked: "What's the matter? You don't like my gift, do you?"

"Oh, no, that's not it. It's beautiful. I love it. It's just that—"

Consuela interrupted her. "I know," she said. "It was really thoughtless of me. I just went into the store and picked it out. I didn't even wrap it myself. I'm so embarrassed. You spent hours and hours creating this masterpiece for me, and all I did was walk in, point, and say, 'I'll take that one.' I'm sorry if I disappointed you. I didn't mean to ruin your birthday."

"No, no," Heather tried to say between her tears. "I was just thinking how you spent so much money on this dress! I could never afford to give you anything as elegant as this! All I did was collect somebody's leftover scraps and sew them together with leftover thread. Recycled garbage is all it is! Momma was going to throw it out, but I took it instead. You spent a fortune on me, and all I gave you was recycled garbage."

"Don't you ever say such a thing!" Consuela commanded. She gently took Heather's head into her hands and made direct eye contact. "Now, listen to me. I wish I had your creativity. This is talent. With a million dollars, I could never purchase anything as marvelous as this quilt. You can't buy talent. You have to be born with it. And this gift is something I will never forget. Thank you. *Thank you.*"

Then suddenly, the two of them collapsed into each other's arms, crying and laughing at the same time, and basking in the unspeakable bond between them. How foolish they had been, each one thinking that the other was disappointed in her birthday offering. They had almost lost sight of what birthday presents and best friends are all about.

The sound of Consuela's parents at the front door startled them.

"We got here just in time—we brought a birthday cake! Come on, you two. Let's celebrate your sixteen years of life!"

Seeing Your Own Story

- With whom do you identify more easily, Heather or Consuela? What was one of the best presents you ever received? What was one of the best presents you ever gave?

Seeing the Faith Story

We often start our prayers this way: "In the name of the Father, the Son, and the Holy Spirit. Amen."

As Catholic Christians, we believe in *one* God who is *three* persons. We call this the Trinity.

Our belief that God exists as the Trinity is central to our faith. And yet, it's a mystery we really cannot explain. We can only provide images. For instance, we might describe the three persons of the Trinity in this way: the One Who Creates All Things (Father), the One Who Redeems All (Son), and the One Who Makes All Things Holy (Spirit). Or we might say the One Who Loves, the One Who Is Loved, and the Energy of Love. When we use these images, we might get a sense of what God is like, but we can never really grasp the whole truth.

We also say that God is love, but we can't completely define love either. Still, we know love when we see it. We can see it in Consuela and Heather's friendship. Each loved the other; and each was loved by the other; and their bond of trust was strong and powerful— almost like a force that was separate from them yet was obviously of them. It was that power of trust that kept them together and helped them be honest, so that their misunderstanding could be resolved.

- We can think of the Blessed Trinity as (1) the Giver, (2) the Receiver, and (3) the Power of Giving. Heather and Consuela's relationship has these same three aspects. How is the Trinity a model for human relationships?

I believe in God . . .

The Best of Both Worlds

When Kent heard the footsteps, he woke up from a nightmare about his father. He looked over groggily at the stranger approaching his bed. Her hair was gray, her dress was brown, and a cross was hanging from her neck.

"Are you Kenton Lehigh?" she asked upon reaching his bedside, her thick Texas accent falling annoyingly on his Ohio ears.

"It's Kent," he answered coldly.

"Hi, Kent, I'm Sr. Emily Schwartz," she said, extending her hand. "I'm one of the hospital chaplains. I just stopped in to see how you are doin' today."

When the patient shook his visitor's hand, he didn't even bother to fake a smile. "Hello, Sister," he mumbled.

"So, what happened to your leg?" the elderly woman asked, studying the apparatus that held the teenager's leg suspended over the bed.

"Motorcycle accident," Kent replied.

"Ouch!" Sister Emily winced. "That must've hurt like the devil!"

"Wasn't any fun," he remarked with sarcasm, "but I'm alive."

"Thanks be to God!" Sister Emily exclaimed. "Thanks be to—"

"Sister, I hate to be rude, but I'm not very religious," Kent interrupted, hoping to cut off any further mention of God's name. "Maybe you should visit someone else—someone who goes to church more than once a year."

"I visit all patients, whether they're Catholics or not, or churchgoers or not," she explained with a wide smile. "But I won't pester you if you really want to be left alone."

"Why don't you just say a quick prayer for me and then come back tomorrow when I'm in a better mood?" Kent suggested. "Besides, my girlfriend's going to be here any minute."

"Fine," the chaplain said. "How about sayin' the Our Father with me?"

He nodded stiffly, then turned away from his visitor as they prayed. When the prayer ended, and Sister Emily reached for his hand to bid him farewell, he quickly wiped a tear from his eye with the corner of the sheet.

"Is somethin' the matter, Kent?" the chaplain asked with obvious concern in her voice, moving to the other side of the sixteen-year-old's bed.

"I hate that prayer, Sister!" he said with quiet anger. "The Our Father makes me think of my dad, who used to slap my mom around when he got drunk, and scream at my little sister when she didn't wait on him hand and foot, and beat me up when I tried to defend them. Then he left town when I was ten." Kent's face was red, his teeth clenched. "If God is a father, I don't want to know him!"

Without a hint of disapproval, Sister Emily took Kent's hand and squeezed it softly. "My parents were killed in a car wreck when I was two, so I never knew either of them," she said. "My granny raised me. At her funeral, I realized that she had been the most lovin' person I'd ever known. If God is love, I told myself that day, then God must be like my granny. And so now, I often pray, 'Our Granny, who art in heaven.' And, you know, my uncle Donald's a great person, too. Sometimes, 'Our Uncle' works well for me."

The teenager with the shattered leg looked up at the elderly woman who was holding his hand. He shook his head and laughed. "Then God's kind of like a cross-dresser, huh? A he or a she, depending on the situation."

Sister Emily chuckled. "I've never thought of it that way, Kent!" She let go of his hand and sat on the arm of a chair. "But since God's neither male nor female, we're free to include the best of both worlds, right? Think of the most lovin', life-givin' person you know, and speak to God as you would to that person."

"My mom's the most generous person I know," Kent said. "She joined Al-Anon four years ago, worked full-time while finishing her BA, and has supported me and my sister all these years without a cent from Dad. How about, 'Our Mother, who art in heaven'?"

"Why not?" the hospital chaplain concurred. "Sounds good to me!" All of a sudden her eyes were twinkling. "And if you should get married and have children of your own one day, will you do me a favor?"

"What?" Kent asked, beginning to like the older woman with the drawl and the cross around her neck.

"Will you make an extra effort to love your kids well so they can say, 'Our Father,' with pride and conviction?"

"It's a deal," he smiled. "But I'll need lots of prayers to help me, Sister."

"Oh, I can pray for you big time," Sister Emily laughed. "My Texas granny brought me up to do everything big time."

Seeing Your Own Story

- Why does Kent's anger at his father stand in the way of his thinking of God as Father? Should Sister Emily have insisted on his appreciating the fatherhood of God, by pointing out to Kent the good qualities of an ideal father?
- When you think of God as Father, what qualities come to mind? When you think of God as Mother, what qualities come to mind? What traits of God are common to both fatherhood and motherhood?

Seeing the Faith Story

Christians believe that God, from whom all life and goodness come, is far too wonderful for us to understand completely or to speak about in clear words and definitions. Where words fail, though, images come to our aid.

In different places, the Bible compares God to a mother who gives birth to and cuddles her babies, to a father who lovingly cares for and guides his children, to a husband who remains faithful to his unfaithful wife, to a woman who bakes bread, and to a woman who throws a party for her neighbors. The Bible presents God in images drawn from our real-life experiences of good and holy people.

When Christians pray, "Our Father," they are speaking to the Person from Whom All Life Comes and to Whom All Life Returns, the First Source of Goodness, Health, Happiness, and Holiness. Parents—both mothers and fathers—are a powerful symbol of this ever creative, life-giving God we believe in. For this reason, Sister Emily encouraged Kent to be comfortable thinking about God as both Father and Mother.

- Do you have an easier time thinking of God as Father or as Mother? Why?
- What other images of God are you familiar with or do you prefer? What do these images tell you about God?

. . . the Father almighty . . .

So, Big Deal!

"Hello."

"Hello, is Yolanda there?"

"Libby! It's me! That's the second time this week you didn't recognize my voice! What's with you, girl?"

"I'm having a bad week."

"You're always having a bad week. What's the deal this time?"

"Fights with my mom, fights at work. It never lets up."

"You know it! Your whole life's a pity party! Good thing you've got so many mess-ups to talk about! Otherwise, my phone life would be one big yawn. Let it all out, honey. Tell Yolanda the latest."

"Okay, okay. Maybe it's not such a big deal. My mom's mad because she found two glass bottles and some number two plastic in the trash. Okay, so, I got lazy and didn't rinse them out and put them in the recycling bins. So, big deal!"

"I thought you cared about the environment. I thought you were queen of the 'save the whales, save the parks, use no artificial preservatives, and keep the natural look' movement. I thought all that was important to you. Heck, you won't even use those spray cans because of the CVCs."

"CFCs."

"Yeah. Whatever. So, something tells me you didn't apologize and do the humble bit to your mom . . ."

"I should have. But when she started talking to me about it, I didn't know she had already examined the trash. She asked me if I remembered to recycle while she was gone all day Saturday, and I said yes. So, I lied. So, big deal! So then she lectured me about the environment; and about my children's children; and about our poor planet and about how it's everyone's responsibility; and about how fish and birds and buffalo have to trust us to do the right things; and about how we are all part of this delicate ecological cycle; and about how everything we do causes ripples, like the ones in a pond that keep moving out; and about how she can't trust me when I lie; and about how all relationships are built on trust. And on and on. So, big deal!"

"So, big mistake. Parents hate lying. It's the worst. To them, it is a big deal. Next thing you know, she'll stop believing everything you say, and she'll be checking up on your every move. We'd better not plan anything sneaky this weekend."

"I won't have time for fun, anyway. I'm working Friday, Saturday, and Sunday. It's going to be awful."

"I thought you loved that job at the card shop. You're working in that fantasyland where every day is just another holiday waiting to happen."

"It's okay, I guess. But I hate this new kid Kermit."

"Kermit? No way! You mean like the frog? Is he dating some pig?"

"A pig would be too good for him."

"Okay, so tell me what's up with this Kermit person."

"He told me he was working on a special order in the back room, so he couldn't come out and help sort the new Mother's Day cards, and the Father's Day cards, and the graduation cards, and all that. And he couldn't wait on the customers when we had five people in the shop, with just me and Mr. Tokarz up front."

"And so . . . ?"

"And so, I found out from Mr. Tokarz that there was no special order! Kermit made it all up! He's just lazy and thinks it's funny when I have to do all the work by myself!"

"Did you tell Mr. Tokarz? What did he say?"

"He didn't believe me. He said that I must have misunderstood Kermit. He said Kermit wouldn't lie. Kermit's his nephew. Mr. Tokarz thinks he's wonderful! He doesn't want to hear any family criticism. So there's nothing I can do."

"Well, what did you say to Kermit?"

"I called him a liar. I told him what he did was wrong. I told him he could hurt the store's business by forcing two clerks to wait on five people. One of them left because she didn't want to wait so long to be helped. Know what he said?"

"'Big deal?'"

"Yeah. How'd you know?"

"Because that's what you say when you're in trouble and you've got nothing else to say."

"No, I don't."

"Oh, yes, you do."

"So, big deal."

"There you go! You just can't help yourself! It's your cop-out whenever you get caught doing something you know you can't get out of."

"I'm still mad that Kermit the Frog lied to me. I mean, he lied right to my face! How can I trust someone who lies? All relationships are built on trust! We're all part of this big circle, just like the fish and the birds and the buffalo, and everything we do has a ripple effect, just like in a pond, and . . . Oh, no! Did you hear that? I'm beginning to sound like my mother!"

"So, big deal!"

Seeing Your Own Story

- What values is Libby's mother trying to teach Libby? Why is it sometimes hard for you—as it is for Libby—to be consistent in living out your values?

- Would most teens lie, like Kermit, to cover themselves? How important is telling the truth to you? Think of a time you told a lie. How did you feel? What happened?

Seeing the Faith Story

All of nature operates on a delicate cycle. As human beings, we are the only creatures who are capable of destroying what God has created for us to enjoy. Every time we are careless or lazy with our trash, or every time we invent something new without investigating the effect it may have on the environment, we threaten creation rather than acting with God as cocreators. Libby's two unrecycled glass bottles and unrecycled number two plastic container by themselves aren't enough to ruin the balance of nature, but when they are added to millions of other unrecycled containers, every day, the sum effect is very destructive. It's like lying: when we lie once, it's easy to lie a second time and a third time, and then who knows what's what? The simple truth is that good choices produce good results, and bad choices produce bad results. God trusts us to be stewards of creation, to treat our inner and outer environment with respect and care. To do otherwise hurts our planet, ourselves, and future generations of human beings.

- Why might people of faith feel a special responsibility to take care of the earth? What do you do to help keep the environment healthy? What can you do better in the future?

. . . *creator of heaven and earth.*

Seeing Double

Dear Gabby,

I have a best friend—let's call her Ken Chang. She's almost part of my family. Ever since we were kids, she's come with my family on vacation. And when the Changs go on vacation, I go with them. I never want anything to come between me and Kenny, or between me and her parents.

But that's the problem. Her father is now my math teacher. And I hate him. I mean, I hate him in school, but I still love him at Kenny's house. I mean, Mr. Chang gives us too much homework, and when it's late, we get points taken off, even if it's only a day late. No other teacher is that strict. And if we don't understand a problem, he takes a poll. If no more than eight of us are confused, he won't explain the problem in class. He makes those of us who need more help come in during a special study hall so he doesn't have to "waste everyone else's time." I mean, the math study hall is a good idea and everything, and he does a good job of explaining things to the five or six of us who are regulars, but it's embarrassing to have to go. The other kids are calling it the Math Dummy Hour.

How can Mr. Chang be that strict at school? He's so much fun at Kenny's. I don't know what to do. It's the first honors math class that has ever given me a problem. I know I can transfer out of it, but I don't want to. That would mess up my whole schedule. I just want things to be normal. I want to be able to like Mr. Chang again, or I want to be able to hate him without guilt, like everyone else in the Math Dummy Hour. It's easy for them to hate him. They don't know what he's really like. I wish I didn't know either. It would be simpler that way. I saw him at a food store last week, and I didn't know whether he was Mr. Chang the teacher, or Mr. Chang, Ken's dad. I didn't know whether I should duck behind the next aisle or give him a hug. How can one man be two different people? Am I seeing double?

Last, but not least, there are now problems between Kenny and me. She's always feeling bad because she never has to go to the study hall. She's never confused. She can solve equations I couldn't begin to understand.

What should I do, Gabby? Please help me!

Seeing Double

» » » « « «

Dear Seeing Double,

I agree you have a problem, but it's in how you're seeing things, not with Mr. Chang. Mr. Chang is preparing you for college. You are in your first difficult math class, and most of the other students in your class are not having as much trouble as you are. I think you have a great set-up. Your teacher has figured out a way to help the less advanced students catch up without holding back the more advanced students. It's not his fault that kids are making fun of the study hall (although I think it's awful when anyone makes fun of another person). Their childish name-calling says more about them than it does about you. See it for what it is and try to ignore it. They may get tired of it if you don't seem to care.

As far as your difficulty with the two Mr. Changs, I advise you to try to like the whole man. Why make things complicated? He's really not two different people. So adjust your vision, and you will stop seeing double. True, you see him in two different places: in Ken's house, which is a fun place, and also in math class, which is a stressful place. But he's not causing the stress in class; he's trying to help you deal with it. He wants you to learn, and he's on your side. He's challenging you in order to help you to grow and develop your skills.

And don't overlook the most obvious possibility, talking to Mr. Chang. Chances are he would be sympathetic to your situation, and it would give you a chance to hear his side of things. I bet you'd walk away feeling a lot better after discussing your problem with him.

Finally, don't let this affect your friendship with Ken! Mr. Chang is one man with two roles to play in your life: your teacher and your best friend's dad. He sounds as if he is doing a great job in both. I bet you'll be able to cope. You have a good thing going with Ken's family.

Best wishes!
Gabby

Seeing Your Own Story

- Which problem do you think was worse for Seeing Double: having to attend Math Dummy Hour, or having to deal with the two roles of Ken's dad? Why?
- Have you had to deal with one person who treated you two different ways in two different situations? If so, what was that like? Do you ever treat the same person two different ways, depending on the situation?

Seeing the Faith Story

In some ways, Jesus is like Mr. Chang. You can look at him and see double.

Jesus has two natures. He is a human being like us, born of a human mother into a human family. He had to be fed and taken care of as a baby. He probably had a group of friends he played with every day, and he probably became giggly with girls when he was a young teen.

Unlike us, Jesus is also divine. He is God. During his time on earth, he knew people's hearts, cured diseases, and walked on water. He rose from the dead and appeared to his friends.

The mystery of the Incarnation is the mystery of one Jesus with two natures, human and divine. Nevertheless, those who knew the earthly Jesus knew only one person; they could not have chosen which Jesus to relate to, the human Jesus or the divine Jesus. For them, and also for us, Jesus is a combination package: he's one person, with two natures.

Similarly, for Seeing Double, Mr. Chang was one person with two distinct roles. The Mr. Chang who challenged his students at school was the same Mr. Chang who also enjoyed spending time with Ken and her friends at home. Gabby encourages Seeing Double to accept the different roles that the one person, Mr. Chang, played in her life.

- Is it easier for you to relate to Jesus the all-powerful and all-knowing God, or to Jesus the human being who once was a teenager like you? Can you appreciate Jesus the combination package, who is both human and divine, or does that make you feel as if you are seeing double?

I believe in Jesus Christ, his only Son, our Lord.

Waiting and Listening

For as long as he could remember, Anthony had dreamt of being a surgeon like his uncle Tony. Since entering high school, he had studied hard and taken all the right courses, in the hope of being accepted into the premed program at the University of Iowa. In the second semester of his senior year, however, his lifelong dream suddenly became a living nightmare.

To begin with, he earned only a C+ in physics during the first semester, and by early February, he was already having more trouble in calculus than he'd ever had in physics. Then in late March, while he was still waiting to hear from the U of I about his application for financial assistance, his second cousin Hope, who was also planning to study medicine, received scholarship offers from Notre Dame and Creighton. And to top everything off, his best friend, Ian, who was skating through chorus and advanced art while Anthony was struggling with physics and calculus, won first place in oral interpretation at the state speech contest in April and was immediately offered a full scholarship in performing arts at Drake University. Was he reaching too high in his dreams? Anthony began to wonder. Was he just too stupid to ace the higher sciences and math? Or was fate against him? Would he always fall flat, no matter what he did or how hard he tried?

By the time May rolled around, Anthony was so consumed by the pressures of grades and self-doubt that he could hardly sleep at night. When he came down with a severe case of mono three weeks before graduation, the family doctor hospitalized him. The first day in a hospital bed, the ailing senior did nothing but cry. Then he slept for the next eighteen hours.

After waking up the following afternoon, Anthony noticed a pile of mail lying on a table next to his bed. Everyone in my class must have written me a get-well note! he thought, laughing as he reached for the bundle, feeling more rested than he had in months. But his laughter stopped short when he recognized his uncle Tony's unmistakable handwriting on the first piece of mail. He dropped everything else and tore open the blue envelope. *"'Happy Birthday'?"* Anthony cried out loud as he read the card. "Gosh! I didn't even remember my own birthday!" Shaking his head in disbelief, he picked up the letter that had fallen from the card and began to read:

Dear Anthony,
  Whenever I think about the day you were named after me, I smile with pride.

Yes, you have made me proud, and not just because you want to pursue a career in medicine. I am proud of you because you have always been a good person. Do you remember the little kid who used to bring home stray cats and dogs and insist that his mother feed them? Or the time you told me—you were all of nine or ten, I think—that you secretly shared your allowance with your little sister because she wasn't old enough to get her own? Or when your mother was sick and you did the family laundry for a month? "That boy's going to be a veterinarian or a priest," I told a friend once, before learning that your dream was to be a surgeon like your uncle.

Well, your uncle's career as a surgeon is about to end, I'm afraid. The shaking in my left hand has gotten so bad lately that I've decided to offer my resignation to the hospital board. I have yet to hear from them, but I'm sure it's only a matter of time.

What backup plans do I have? None, but I do believe that God is calling me, and saying yes to that call is more important than making my own plans, anyway. If Mary was only a teenager when she said yes to God's call to be the mother of Jesus, then there's hope for this old surgeon with Parkinson's disease. I'll just have to wait and listen for the call.

I will be in Davenport for your graduation, Anthony. Until then, take care of yourself.

Happy birthday! Please pray for me as I face an unknown future, and I'll pray for you as you embark on your dreams.

Love,
Uncle Tony

When Anthony finished his uncle's letter, he put the rest of the birthday mail back on the table without opening it. There was just too much to think about right now. He closed his eyes and thanked God that Uncle Tony would be there for his graduation. "Hail Mary, full of grace," the teenager prayed fervently, wondering whether God had a surprising call in store for him, too.

Seeing Your Own Story

- If you were Uncle Tony, and Anthony asked you for your honest opinion, would you encourage him to consider other career possibilities, or simply urge him to stick with his original dream, no matter what? Why?
- Why do you think Uncle Tony mentioned how young Mary was when she was called to be the mother of Jesus? Do you think Mary experienced any doubts or fears when she received her call? Why or why not?

Seeing the Faith Story

The Bible tells us that when God called Mary to be the mother of Jesus, she said: "I am your servant. Your will be done" (adapted from Luke 1:38). In her openness to God's call, Mary set an example that Christians have tried to imitate for many centuries.

Ancient Christian writers insisted that Mary's faith in God was even more wonderful than her miraculous pregnancy. Because of her faith in God's goodness, Jesus took on our flesh, became part of our history, and renewed our world.

In his letter, Uncle Tony told Anthony that even the best-laid plans sometimes fail. In light of this possibility, only one thing can be counted on: God's love. We follow Mary, the mother of Jesus, when we trust in God's love, especially when we are uncertain or afraid. Great things happen when God is given room to work in our life!

- Do you believe that people of all ages are truly called by God to do certain things? Why or why not?
- What do your talents and dreams suggest about your future vocation? What have your family and friends encouraged you to think about? What possibilities have school, work, and extracurricular activities introduced you to? Is it hard to believe that God may be providing direction for you through these things?

He was conceived by the power of the Holy Spirit and born of the Virgin Mary.

A New Way to Live and Die

"Hey, Rita."

"Yeah?"

"Have you ever been to a funeral home before?"

"Yeah—when my grandfather died. But this is different, Holly."

"How's it different?"

"This funeral's for a teenager. My grandfather was old. At his funeral, everyone was smiling and laughing and telling jokes and being happy. I've never seen anyone my age in a coffin before."

"Well, I didn't really even know Mario. I just know some of his friends, and his sister. I wanted to come to the funeral for her. She's really broken up about this. So am I—and I didn't even know the guy."

"Well, I didn't either, but my mother was a friend of his mother's sister or cousin or something. It's just horrible when something like this happens. I cried when I heard the news. But he looks peaceful now. He must be in a better place."

"What makes you so sure? You make it sound as if he were a little angel all his life. You don't know his friends, Rita. They've done some pretty bad things. They are no saints, I can tell you that. I don't think any of them deserve to be in the church basement, never mind heaven!"

"Holly! Come on! Who made you the judge? Besides, heaven's a gift. No one deserves it."

"Oh, yeah. You're talking about salvation. Like the preachers on TV. 'Our salvation is a gift from God,' right? We actually deserve to burn in hell because we're bad, and God is mean and hateful, and we have to be punished. But Jesus didn't want us to be punished, right? So he took the blame for us, and that's why he got crucified, and God called it even so now we can all go to heaven."

"Holly! Are you serious? This is a joke, right?"

"What?"

"You don't really believe that!"

"That's what the preachers say, right?"

"Well, yes and no. A little bit right, but majorly wrong. The whole bit about the angry, nasty God who had to punish someone, so he picked Jesus, is a bit much."

"So then why did Jesus die?"

"I think it's more complicated than that. Jesus didn't come just to die. He came to show us the right way to live. You know, to set us straight. And because he was good and pure, some people in power decided to get rid of him."

"So, Jesus was killed because he was good. Why would people want to kill a good person?"

"I don't know. Why was Abraham Lincoln shot? Why was Martin Luther King Jr. shot? Why was Archbishop Oscar Romero shot? People get jealous, they think someone has too much power, they get violent. I don't know. It's stupid. Look at the peer pressure in school. Look what happens if someone doesn't want to drink or do drugs or cheat or have sex. If you want to be good and do the right thing, people are going to dislike you. As little kids, they make fun of you. When they get older, they beat you up or kill you. I don't know why. The whole thing is stupid, but that's what happens."

"But Mario was no martyr. And his friends are no Abraham Lincoln! They drink, they smoke, they do drugs. Maybe they steal stuff. Maybe they've even raped someone. You don't know! Rita, if people like that can go to heaven, then why not do whatever you want? Maybe I'll start sinning more often!"

"Holly, I can't believe you. You said you really didn't know Mario, yet you're positive he didn't make it to heaven. I'm not so sure. Maybe if we grow up poor and our parents beat us up and we get sexually abused, we're going to have more problems and do some pretty bad things. You can't judge what life was like for Mario. You don't even know yourself what he did. You're just making all this up to see what I will say. Here's what I think: I think we should let God judge—the loving God who sent Jesus to help us learn to live better and die better."

"Rita, how did you learn all this stuff? Did you have, like, a religious experience or something?"

"No! I just pay attention in church once in a while. And I guess I read the bulletin. And sometimes I hear my mom and her friends talking about this kind of stuff during their prayer group. I don't listen to them all the time, but once in a while, it's fun to eavesdrop."

"Well, I hope Mario's friends learn from this."

"Learn what?"

"You know, that life doesn't go on forever, and that we should be paying close attention to what we choose to do while we're alive."

"I hope I learn that, too. I hope we all do. That's why Jesus came, to show us a new way to live and die."

Seeing Your Own Story

- Do you think it was strange for Holly and Rita to have that conversation at a funeral home? Was it disrespectful to Mario?
- Have you ever been to anyone's funeral? Have you ever been to the funeral of a

young person? If you have been to a funeral, did you spend any time thinking about heaven?

Seeing the Faith Story

Human beings know about sin, suffering, and death. Yet deep down, they long for lasting happiness. The story of Adam and Eve grapples with this tension. After experiencing perfect happiness in the Garden of Eden, Adam and Eve eat from the forbidden tree—and their lives change for the worse. "Who will save us from our troubles?" they cry out. This question has echoed thoughout history.

Christians believe that Jesus is the "new Adam," the one who came to deliver human beings from their troubles, the one who came to save them from sin.

As Rita tried to explain to Holly, our salvation from sin, suffering, and death comes from Jesus, as a free gift. Our rightful response to that gift is to do our best to live and die the way Jesus showed us.

- Which point of view do you relate to more: Holly's idea of an angry God punishing the wicked, or Rita's idea of salvation as a free gift from Jesus? What do you think it means to believe that Jesus came to save you?

He suffered under Pontius Pilate, was crucified, died, and was buried.

Back from the Dead

20 May

Dear Aaron,

After I got your letter yesterday, I couldn't keep my mind on my classes. All I could think about was how depressed I was when I started drug treatment two summers ago. You sound depressed, too. What can I tell you except to stick with it? You'll be happier if you tough it out now. If you don't face your demons today, they'll be meaner demons tomorrow.

Two years ago, everybody knew that I was a slave to cocaine. Even I knew it, but I wouldn't admit it. I thought I was on top of the world and no one could touch me— even though I was barely passing my classes and was stealing from my family to support my habit. Besides, all my friends were junkies.

The night I was arrested, I was racing ninety-five miles per hour down the highway, hoping to push the speedometer on Dad's '72 Dart past one hundred. I didn't care that my girlfriend, Patrice, was with me; that she was screaming for me to slow down; or that the red lights flashing in the rearview mirror were closing in on me. "No one's ever caught me before, and no one'll catch me tonight!" I bragged, higher on stupidity than I was on coke. When the car rolled into the ditch, and Patrice's face smashed into the dash, I still didn't think there was anything wrong. "It's just a bad dream," I assured myself. "I always wake up and find myself safe and sound in bed."

Well, I woke up five days later in a hospital bed. My left leg was missing below the knee; Patrice's funeral had already come and gone; and Patrice's parents were suing my dad for negligence, because he owned the wrecked car. If I had once felt on top of the world, I was now in the pits of hell.

The first angel appeared when Patrice's parents dropped their suit after I agreed to go for treatment. I still don't understand why they were so generous. If I'd lost a daughter because of some drug-snorting idiot, I'd have wanted his head on a platter. I wrote them a letter of apology on the anniversary of Patrice's death, but I didn't get an answer from them. I probably never will.

The second angel appeared at the treatment center. The chaplain, Rev. Renee Liston, assured me that God didn't hate me, but also informed me that I wasn't the center of the world. "You're the perfect example of the addictive personality," she said. "Self-will run riot." Whenever I resisted the program, she told me to get off my throne and give it back to God. After I did my fifth step with her and admitted the many things I'd done wrong, she hugged me and told me how much God loves an honest heart. "How can God love a screwup like me?" I cried on her shoulder. "God loves anyone who's real," she answered. "When you were hiding your hurts behind drugs, God's love just couldn't get through."

The third angel appeared in the person of my sponsor. I haven't taken a drink of alcohol or a snort of coke in almost two years, and it's because Ike has always been there when I've been too weak to resist temptation and needed someone to talk to. He hasn't judged me, but he hasn't fallen for my excuses, either.

On my birthday, Ike took me on a trip to the Black Hills to celebrate my sobriety. On crutches, looking out over the pine-covered hills, listening to the river babbling below me, I felt a rush I'd never gotten from drugs. I was so overcome, I had to sit down. When I tried to explain what was happening to me, Ike smiled. "Only your Higher Power can really fill you with life, Casey. Booze and drugs are a one-way ticket to death."

And so you see, Aaron, I'm on my way back from the dead! If I could bring Patrice back with me, I would. The only way I can honor her memory now is to become an angel for someone else. I want to be your friend. As a true friend, I won't lie. There's no easy way out of the treatment center, no easy way to face your shortcomings and make a new start. But if you're willing to do the hard work, I'll stand with you to the very end.

Wishing you the very best,
Casey

Seeing Your Own Story

- What did Casey's chaplain mean by telling him to get off the throne and give it back to God? Was Casey too harsh when he told Aaron that he would only be Aaron's "angel" if Aaron agreed to be honest and do the hard work of recovery?
- Do you agree with those who belong to Alcoholics Anonymous and Al-Anon when they say that only a "higher power" can deliver a person from addiction? Why is it difficult for human beings to turn the steering wheel of life over to God?

Seeing the Faith Story

Christians believe that after his death on the cross, Jesus rose from the dead. This belief is the very heart of Christian faith. "If Christ has not been raised," the Bible tells us, "your faith is futile."

In Jesus' victory over death, God has delivered creation from the destructive power of sin and suffering. Because they are baptized into the Risen Christ, Christians believe that they stand with Jesus on the threshold of a new era of history, an era in which God is gradually breaking in and transforming the world.

We see evidence of this transformation in small and large ways: in the mutual forgiveness of long-time enemies, in the change of heart of oppressors, in the hard-earned sober lifestyle of drug addicts like Casey and Aaron, in the steady support of family and friends, and in the quiet surrender of an elderly person to death. Christians see in this pattern of transformation a reflection of Jesus' paschal mystery—that is, of Jesus' life, death, and Resurrection. Whenever we die to selfishness and sinful habits, we share in Jesus' victory; and when we die bodily, we also share in Jesus' victory

In all the ups and downs of life, the Risen Christ is our sure hope that no evil, however great, can undo the great good God is intent on doing: saving the world!

- Have you noticed the pattern of death and resurrection in your personal life—of rising up from pain, sadness, or sin to renewed joy and greater wisdom? Do you see evidence of this pattern in your family history? in your community or in the world? Share your thoughts on this topic with someone else.

He descended into hell. On the third day he rose again.

The Light at the End of the Tunnel

"I'm very nervous sitting here in front of you, but at the same time, I have many important things to say. When Ms. Thomas-Jones invited me, several weeks ago, to share my experiences with you, at first, I said no. Then I remembered how much my grandpa's words helped me before surgery: 'I've been under the knife more times than a Thanksgiving turkey. When the doctor puts me to sleep, I just tell myself that God's in charge of the operation, and I pray for a good dream!' We can learn a lot by listening to others, don't you think? But if others are afraid to speak out, we have to learn everything for ourselves. So, it's my turn to speak out today, to share with you the amazing things I've discovered.

"As some of you know, my parents and I discussed the brain surgery for many months before I agreed to it. We knew it would be a big risk, but we figured that the hoped-for result was well worth the gamble. If the surgeons could finally relieve the shaking in my arms, then maybe I could sleep at night without medication and even start feeding and dressing myself again. I would be still confined to a wheelchair, but much less dependent on my family.

"My biggest fear before surgery was not the 20 percent chance that the shaking would be worse after the operation, but the 10 percent chance that I wouldn't survive the procedure. I'm only seventeen years old, I told myself. There's so much to see and do in this world, even from a wheelchair! What if I die? Am I ready?

"The night before I went to the hospital, I had a bad dream: I was lying peacefully in a black coffin, and all my relatives and friends were gathered around me, telling stories.

"'Did you know that Zach was jealous of me?' my younger brother told the others. 'He was jealous because I could run up the stairs and play baseball with my friends and ride a bike. He spat food in my face one day at lunch because I was going to the gym to shoot hoops with my friends instead of staying home to play computer games with him.'

"'Sounds just like Zachary John!' my mom laughed. 'You know, he was so mad at me once for picking him up late after school that he called me a name I won't repeat and said he hated me. It hurt for a whole week.'

"'Did I ever tell you,' Dad joined in, 'about the time I came home and found Zach bleeding in the bathroom? He'd taken a knife from the kitchen and was stabbing at his neck with his shaky hand, hoping to do himself in. It's hard to imagine a fifteen-year-old wanting to die, isn't it?'

"'And did I tell you that Zach accused me once of just *pretending* to be his friend?' my buddy Randy said. '"You're embarrassed to be seen with me, aren't you?" he yelled at me one day after having a seizure in class.'

"'Oh, he told me dozens of times he should never've been born,' my mother chimed in again. 'God's Big Mistake, he called himself.'

"That awful dream! All those terrible voices! I couldn't get them out of my head when I was being wheeled to the surgery room. They were like fingers pointing at me, telling me things I didn't want to remember. All of a sudden, I was more afraid than ever: What if I died? What would God do to me? Then I thought of my grandpa's advice, and I quickly told God I was sorry and begged for a good dream. My prayer was answered: I dreamt I was floating above the operating table, looking down a long tunnel with a bright light at the end, happy and free at last. Just as I was about to take an angel's hand, I fell back. 'Not this time, Zach,' a voice said as the light gradually disappeared. 'There's more for you to do on earth.'

"So, here I am today, telling you what I've learned about life by bumping up against death. First, life passes, and we are given only so many chances to make something of ourselves. We can spend the time complaining about what we don't have, or we can make the best of what we do have. I have enough to be happy, even if I'll never drive a car or play basketball.

"Second, the biggest mistake we can make in life is thinking our life's a mistake. We're here for a reason, and the world needs our gifts, no matter how big or small. I don't know exactly what God wants me to do. Maybe I'm just supposed to talk this one time to Ms. Thomas-Jones's religious education class.

"Third, we need to take responsibility for ourselves. If we do dumb or hurtful things, we need to apologize for them and learn from them. Since my operation, I've apologized to all my family and friends and made a new start.

"Finally, things don't always turn out the way we want. My arms still tremble, and I still need my parents' help to get around. But you know, my parents need me, too: they need my love and my thanks. The world would be a far better place if all of us asked for help when we needed it and offered help when we could."

Seeing Your Own Story

- Why was Zach nervous about sharing his experience with the religious education class? Why did he finally agree to do so? Which of the four things he has learned about life do you think is most important?

- Why is it difficult for us to accept the limits that life imposes on us? Why is it often easier to be angry about our shortcomings than to be thankful for our gifts and abilities?

Seeing the Faith Story

Like Zach, others who have had a near-death experience often tell of going through a life review and asking questions like: What have I lived for? Whom have I hurt or helped? What have I done or left undone? In the depths of the soul, we are aware of our basic responsibility to use our human freedom well. Christians believe that God created us with intelligence and free will, and that we will be asked at death to give an accounting of how well or poorly we have lived.

The idea of final judgment can be frightening. But we don't have to wait to be on our deathbed to do a life review. We can begin today by comparing our life with the example of Jesus' life in the Gospels. If we live like Jesus, we can be sure that we will die like Jesus: beloved of God and invited to share in the fullness of God's life. There is no reason to live in fear of the final judgment if we try to live with faith, hope, and love every day.

- If you could change one thing about your past, what would it be? Name one specific thing you have learned from your past that helps you to make better choices today.

He ascended into heaven and is seated at the right hand of the Father. He will come again to judge the living and the dead.

Enjoying the Differences

From: schwartzkopfj@easternhs.edu
Sent: Friday, 20 December, 11:15 a.m.
To: quentinp@riversidehs.edu
Subject: Merry Christmas

Dear Quentin,

I can't believe we've never met. We've been e-mail pals for so long that it seems I've known you all my life. When you sent me Happy Hanukkah greetings a couple of weeks ago, even my grandpapa wasn't surprised. "Quentin always remembers, doesn't he?" he remarked on our way to temple. "Yeah," I said, "he's a good friend." "Maybe Christians and Jews are finally learning to get along," Grandpapa smiled. "Quentin and I are doing our best," I assured him.

Whenever we celebrate Hanukkah, Grandpapa tells me all over again about the day his parents were dragged out of their house in Berlin. It was December of 1941, the first day of Hanukkah. He was only eleven then, and he was hidden inside a mattress in the attic with his sister Miriam. After escaping to the United States the next spring with another Jewish family, he learned that my great-grandparents had died at Dachau. There are tears in Grandpapa's eyes whenever he mentions Dachau. Sometimes, I think it would be better if he tried to forget the whole thing, but every year, he tells me the whole story again.

It scares me to think that a modern nation could incinerate millions of human beings like garbage—and not just Jews, but gypsies, priests, handicapped people, and gays as well. Why such hatred? Aren't we all children of the same God? As you celebrate Christmas this year, will you ask God to fill every Christian heart with the love that your Jesus always spoke about? During Hanukkah, I asked God to fill every Jewish heart with the love mentioned in the Book of Leviticus: "You shall love your neighbor as yourself." Without this kind of love, the whole world could easily become a concentration camp, couldn't it? And then no one would be safe.

I'm sorry about this dreary letter, but the holidays have always been a bittersweet time for the Schwartzkopfs, even though Hanukkah is supposed to be a time of rejoicing for us. I do wish you a very merry Christmas, Quentin. Thanks for your letters and your friendship. May the spirit of the holidays fill us both with happiness and peace.

Your friend,
Jonah

» » » « « «

From: quentinp@riversidehs.edu
Sent: Friday, 20 December, 3:05 p.m.
To: schwartzkopfj@easternhs.edu
Subject: Apology Accepted

Dear Jonah,

You really didn't have to apologize for your letter. I'm glad you shared the story about your grandpapa with me. It's no wonder Hanukkah is a bittersweet time for your family. How could it not be, even if other Jewish families are rejoicing? Who says that everyone has to celebrate in the same way? The Jacksons down the street, even though they're Christians, celebrate Kwanza every year as well as Christmas, and my own family celebrates Mom and Dad's anniversary every Christmas Eve as well as Jesus' birth —not the anniversary of their wedding, but the anniversary of their first meeting.

During dinner every December 24, my dad tells us about the night he met my mom when he stopped to pull her car out of a snowdrift. Every year, Mom blushes as if the two of them were only now meeting for the first time. What would Christmas Eve be for my family without Dad's smiles and Mom's blushing? I'm sure we'd still remember what other Christians remember, but the day would feel very different. And your Hanukkah would be very different without your grandpapa's tears. Memories are what make holidays special times.

In French class, we learned a new saying the other day: Vive la différence! Yes, enjoy the differences—it's what God wants, I believe. I'm glad to have a Jewish friend to celebrate the holidays with, and I thank you for giving me the greatest gift I'll get this Christmas: the story about your grandpapa. May God bless us both and everyone we love!

Later,
Quentin

Seeing Your Own Story

- Would it be better for Jonah's grandfather to try to "forget the whole thing" and just enjoy the holidays, as Jonah sadly suggested in his e-mail? Do you think that the story Quentin's father tells every Christmas Eve makes the story of Jesus' birth seem any less important?

- What are some of the tensions that exist between people of different religions? Are you aware of any efforts by religious people to understand one another better or to work together for a common purpose?

Seeing the Faith Story

Human beings, in their quest for true happiness, follow many different paths, as Quentin rightly pointed out to his friend Jonah. One obvious sign of these different paths is the variety of religions in the world today—even the variety of churches among Jesus' followers. Although these differences have at times posed a threat to the human community, they also can enrich that community.

In the history of the Christian church, there has been a struggle to promote the unity of believers while respecting the differences among them. As Christians face this difficult challenge, they turn to the Holy Spirit for guidance and strength. Why? Because Christians believe that the Spirit is the source of both the church's unity and the church's variety of gifts. Without the Spirit, there can be no church, no Body of Christ on earth, and no holy people of God.

Jesus compares the Holy Spirit to the wind that blows freely over the earth. As we cannot see where the wind comes from or where it goes, so we cannot see the wondrous movement of the Holy Spirit or say with certainty where or how the Spirit will act. We can be sure of this much: that the Holy Spirit wants what is best for each person and for the whole world. Variety *and* unity are both marks of the Spirit's presence.

- How might the Holy Spirit be working in your life right now to help you to appreciate the variety and wonder of your unique gifts? of the unique gifts of others? How might the Holy Spirit be pushing you right now to work for greater harmony or understanding between yourself and an estranged friend or relative?

I believe in the Holy Spirit . . .

A Glorious Night
for an Eclipse

"Oh, no! It's tonight! The lunar eclipse!"

"So what?" Ivy asked, wondering what the problem was.

Her mom looked up from the newspaper and frowned. "It's just that I love lunar eclipses, and they only come along once in a while. But tonight's going to be so busy. Chet and Brenda are both working after school, then Brenda's got a youth group meeting, Dad's seeing a client, and somebody's doing something else I can't remember. I guess I'll have to watch it on the run."

Ivy was happy at the thought of being alone in the house. It would be a great night to surf the Internet—she'd have the computer all to herself.

But things didn't turn out that way. Ivy was asked to baby-sit at the Soklers' after school, and as soon as she got home from there, her mom asked her to throw in the spaghetti when the water started to boil, and to heat up some sauce from the freezer. Ivy knew everyone would be eating in shifts that night, and she realized she might be the only one around to do the dishes.

Dad came home with Brenda, but Chet wouldn't get off work for another hour. Brenda grabbed a banana and went out the door with Mom, who stopped in the driveway to look up at the sky.

"Oh, honey, look! What a glorious night for an eclipse! It's starting!"

Ivy reluctantly went out the door with her dad.

"You need to get Brenda over to the church for her meeting," he told his wife. "The sooner you go, the sooner you can come back." When Ivy's mom waved good-bye, Ivy's dad didn't take his eyes off the moon. "Ivy, see that sliver of darkness? The shadow of the earth is going to move across the moon, and the arc of darkness will move across the moon until the moon is completely covered. Then the shadow will go across to the other side, and the moon will grow bright again."

"And you can watch a lunar eclipse all night," a new voice added. "You can't watch a solar eclipse without hurting your eyes. But there's no danger with the moon."

Ivy and her dad turned toward the new voice. It came from their next-door neighbor. "Hi, Mrs. Sokler," Ivy said politely. "I didn't know you liked lunar eclipses, too."

"I had forgotten all about the eclipse! I just came out to give you your baby-sitting money, as I promised. I'm glad I heard you folks talking about it."

Ivy and her dad went back in and ate some supper. Sooner than expected, her mother returned and announced: "The eclipse is well under way! You can really see the shadow now!" She went back out as quickly as she had entered.

Ivy and her dad ran back out to look. Mrs. Sokler was sitting on a lawn chair, all bundled up with a blanket and a thermos of hot tea.

"I'd better go see my client." Ivy's dad was the next one to leave.

Ivy and her mom watched for a while, and then went back in to finish supper. Soon, Chet came through the door. "Mom! Ivy! Come look at the eclipse! It's really coming along!"

All three of them gathered outside and watched. It was so amazing, they just stood in silence.

"Hey, Mom, my clarinet lesson!" Chet blurted out, and the two of them were off again.

Ivy went back in to clean up the dishes and then start up the computer. But on her way from the kitchen to the computer, she had to pass the front door, and somehow that eclipse was calling to her. After all, she did think it was kind of neat. So, she went out and stood near Mrs. Sokler. She couldn't believe this woman was going to sit there all evening and just watch the moon. "I wonder whether my sister remembered about the eclipse?" Mrs. Sokler thought out loud.

"Why don't you call her?" Ivy asked.

"I tried earlier, but the line was busy. I don't want to go inside to use the phone now that the eclipse has started."

"Hey, I'll get our cordless phone. You can use it, and talk to her from your chair." Ivy was in and out in no time, and Mrs. Sokler was very grateful. She had just dialed the number when Ivy's mom came back again, this time with Brenda.

"Oh, look how far the shadow has moved!" Ivy's mom said.

"We were all watching it at Saint Veronica's," Brenda told everyone.

"Does anyone want any spaghetti?" Ivy asked.

"Yes, I'm starved!" Brenda answered, and she followed Ivy into the house.

Just then, the phone rang. Ivy went to answer it, but then she remembered that the handset was outside with Mrs. Sokler. She looked outside and saw that her dad had come back from his appointment. He and her mom were standing there next to Mrs. Sokler, who was again talking on the phone. "How strange," she thought. "Our phone rings, and it's for our next-door neighbor." Ivy almost went upstairs to dive into cyberspace, but she wanted to take just one more peek at the moon. So she grabbed a quilt and an afghan and went outside. The afghan she wrapped around herself; the quilt she gave to her parents.

The moon was completely covered by then, and seemed to be orange. Not very bright at all, but still visible.

Ivy's dad said: "I'd better go get Chet. Will that be it for the night?"

"I hope so," said his wife. "Then it's just us and the moon."

By the time he and Chet returned, there were five lawn chairs set up near Mrs. Sokler. Ivy, Brenda, and their mom were all bundled up, eating popcorn and taking turns calling up all their friends to talk about the moon. Chet and Ivy's dad fell into the empty chairs. It was a glorious night for an eclipse.

Seeing Your Own Story

- At first, Ivy wasn't interested in the eclipse. But by the end of the evening, she was sitting outside watching it, calling up her friends. What changed her mind?
- Enthusiasm about something can be contagious. What is something that used to be uninteresting to you, but now is significant in your life? Who or what helped change your mind about it?

Seeing the Faith Story

What a busy night at Ivy's house! So many people running in and out! And yet, that lunar eclipse kept drawing people together. It kept calling for everyone's attention. There was so much enthusiasm that even Ivy had to come along and check it out. Eventually, she was glad she did.

The Catholic church is like that.

The church reflects the light of Jesus, just as the moon reflects the light of the sun. The light of Jesus draws people from all over, just as the eclipse did.

Some people think that the church is just a building, but more accurately, it is the people of God. All of us have busy lives, coming and going and doing different things, but Jesus keeps calling us. Whenever we are in the darkness, Jesus calls us to the light.

Faith is contagious. We catch it from those around us. It's like the enthusiasm for the eclipse that Ivy couldn't resist. Pretty soon, she was sitting outside on a lawn chair, watching it and eating popcorn and talking on the phone. When we gather as church to worship each weekend, we experience the reflection of Jesus' light, so that we can bring that light to the rest of the world.

- How do you feel about the church? If you are a member of a parish, what good things have you experienced there? If you are not a member of a parish, what kinds of things at a church might interest you?

. . . the holy catholic Church . . .

My Own Special Saints in Heaven

Dear Diary,

I just got back from Grandma's house again. This is the third time since the funeral. The first time was hard, but now, it's not so hard anymore.

At first, I was afraid it would be eerie going in there. I thought it was her stuff, and so we shouldn't be trespassing. But Mom used to live there, so it's kind of her house, too. And it's sort of neat to discover things I never knew about Grandma, or to remember things I had forgotten about her.

For example, we found some old newspaper clippings from when she was in community theater. I never knew she acted! (I never knew they had community theater so long ago!) Mom says it's in our blood. Maybe that means some day, my dream will come true, and I'll get a part in a school play.

I also saw a picture of her when she was a teenager. I couldn't believe it. I thought I was looking at myself! It was like a photo of me with strange hair and an old-style dress!

I used to think I looked like my dad's side of the family, but not anymore!

And I found a little picture I embroidered for her once. I had forgotten all about it! She taught me to sew, and so, I embroidered her a picture of a sewing basket, with spools of thread and a pincushion. She used to tell me always to take tiny stitches. If my stitches were too big, she'd laugh and say I was sewing like a shoemaker. (I guess shoemakers use big stitches.)

I guess what I've discovered is that being in her house isn't eerie at all. In fact, it's kind of comforting. I feel her presence there. It still smells like her a little, and it seems as if she is still teaching me things. I think she's saying that it's all right now. That the suffering is over, the cancer is gone, and she's happy now. She's with Grandpa, and they're both watching me, and I can connect with them in a spiritual way. I can almost just close my eyes and think of her, and I sort of get a sense of what advice she'd be giving me if she were here.

I know Mom eventually has to sell the house, but in the meantime, I have really enjoyed the visits there, remembering both Grandma and Grandpa. I didn't think it would feel like this. I thought it would be sad and scary, and weird. But it's not. It's nice. It seems I have my own special saints in heaven to talk with.

Till next time,
Joy

Seeing Your Own Story

- Do you think that the connection Joy perceives with her grandmother is real? Or do you think Joy just feels better if she pretends there is a heavenly connection?
- What physical characteristics have you observed in your friends that they share with their parents or grandparents? What talents, preferences, or tastes do they share? What are some characteristics you share with your own parents or grandparents?

Seeing the Faith Story

As Joy discovered, people find comfort in the Christian belief in the communion of saints, the belief that we are still connected with our loved ones after they die. Death does not separate us or break the bond between us. We remain united by our love for one another and by the power of the Holy Spirit. The Spirit lives in each of us, giving us the promise and hope of everlasting life. Christians believe that death is not the end of life; it's just the end of life as we know it on earth.

Because of the Holy Spirit, human life never ends, even if it changes dramatically. Because of the Spirit, we are all connected. Because of the Spirit, we form a type of eternal community—a communion of saints. The church gives some saints titles and recognizes them in an official way. You may have heard of Saint Joseph, Saint Elizabeth, Saint Stephen, or Saint Bernadette. We also believe that heaven is filled with saints who are not so famous. You are related to many of them.

- Do you feel a connection to any friend or relative who has died? If so, how do you describe that connection? How has it helped your life?
- Why are saints important in the lives of Christians? Do you feel connected to or inspired by the life of a particular saint?

. . . the communion of saints . . .

A Little Bit of Heaven

Geraldo was so tired after his first week of painting houses and repairing roofs in the hot sun that he fell asleep before his head even hit the pillow. He was dreaming about his air-conditioned home back in Albuquerque when someone tugged at his shoulder and called his name.

"Geraldo," a voice said. "Wake up! I need your help."

"What?" Geraldo answered groggily, struggling to recognize the voice. He opened his eyes, and saw the now-familiar face of Dr. Jean-Michel Plasson. "Geraldo, hurry! Get some clothes on," the doctor urged him. "We've got to get over to the Jeffersons' pronto. Edna's water just broke. Her husband's waiting outside in his pickup."

Hardly able to put one foot in front of the other, Geraldo slowly pulled on his jeans and T-shirt, pulled a comb through his stubborn curls, and stumbled to the bathroom to brush his teeth. Dr. Plasson was already in the battered half-ton pickup by the time Geraldo found his way through the front door. Geraldo ran down the porch steps toward the glaring headlights, embarrassed by his initial slow, begrudging response. Within ten minutes, the trio pulled into the Jeffersons' rut-scarred driveway and raced into the three-room shack.

An hour later, Geraldo was sitting alone on the front porch, hardly able to believe that he had just witnessed the messy birth of a baby. Being a "medical assistant" had been the farthest thing from his mind when he'd volunteered to go to Kentucky to repair the houses of poor people in the Appalachians. Between his junior and senior years in high school and still not knowing what he wanted to do with his life, Geraldo had jumped at the chance to get away from "boring Albuquerque" for the summer. Now, he was having second thoughts: the hot Kentucky sun, the strange accents, the run-down houses, the outdoor bathrooms, the huge families— Gosh! the Jeffersons now had five children! How could they afford another hungry mouth?

The teenager's depressing thoughts were interrupted when Mr. Jefferson came out of the house and took a seat on the steps beside him. He pulled a long red handkerchief from his patched overalls and wiped the sweat from his forehead.

"What a beautiful little girl!" he remarked proudly. "We just named her Jean Michelle, after the good doctor. Can't wait to show her to the kinfolk."

"Yeah, she's really beautiful," Geraldo lied, remembering nothing but the bloody mess and the huge, dripping umbilical cord.

"And what a pretty Kentucky night to bring her into the world," Mr. Jefferson went on. "The sky so full of stars, that little breeze from the northwest, the frogs singing in the ponds. A little bit of heaven, don't you think, Harold?"

Geraldo had corrected Mr. Jefferson's mispronunciation twice before, so he didn't bother this time. "Yeah, it's a beautiful night," he replied halfheartedly, thinking of the cool, dry nights of New Mexico.

"When I get to heaven," the fifth-time father continued, "I hope it'll be a lot like Kentucky. And I hope to see you and the good doctor there, too. We can talk about this night again and again and thank God in person for all the good things we had on earth."

Sick of hearing about the wonders of backwoods Kentucky, the sixteen-year-old spoke up, a note of defiance in his voice. "I always thought heaven would be like the Sangre de Cristo Mountains in New Mexico," he said, "with big, *new* cottages and *lots* of food and *indoor* plumbing!"

"Why not, Harold?" exclaimed Mr. Jefferson, slapping his knee and laughing. "I wouldn't mind spending my heaven anywhere as long as I had Jesus and my family and my friends with me."

What's the secret of this man's happiness? Geraldo wondered silently, shaking his head in disbelief, almost in envy.

"You know, Harold," the Kentuckian said, turning to face his younger companion, "you might be right about heaven being in New Mexico. After all, God sent you from New Mexico to help me and Edna and the kids out, right?"

Geraldo smiled for the first time that night. How odd to be discussing heaven with a man who didn't know the difference between Geraldo and Harold, yet who was probably the happiest and wisest person the teenager had ever met! As Geraldo stared off in to the dark and humid Kentucky night, he wondered what other surprises the summer held in store for him.

Seeing Your Own Story

- Geraldo clearly had mixed reasons for volunteering to go to Kentucky. How can a person agree to something very serious—for example, a career, a religious commitment, or a marriage—with a mixture of noble and not-so-noble motivations?
- Some thinkers claim that the poor Christians of Africa and South America will eventually have to come north to proclaim the gospel to the rich industrialized nations of Europe and North America. What do poor people have to teach rich people about life and faith? Why are wealth and possessions sometimes a barrier to Christian living?

Seeing the Faith Story

Christians believe that the life we are now living is just the beginning of the story. Death will not be the final chapter. Just as Jesus was raised from the dead by the power of the living God, so we who share Jesus' baptism and follow Jesus' example will be raised from the dead and share in the unending life of the Trinity.

Being at one with God and one another is the human heart's deepest desire, as Mr. Jefferson rightly suggested to Geraldo. We must still cooperate with the Holy Spirit in making this earth a home for true peace, justice, and holiness, but at the same time, we can look forward with hope to the life of heaven, a life that will not be marked by sickness, poverty, suffering, or death.

By remembering that our life on earth is only temporary, we can learn to choose what is truly important. Like Geraldo, we might be surprised when we look below the surface of things and find out where life's "true riches" are found.

- Are you aware of a longing in your heart for a richer, more satisfying life, for an end to any present loneliness or pain or frustration? Do you understand why Saint Augustine wrote, "Our hearts are restless, O God, until they rest in you"? Try to express this insight in your own words.

. . . the forgiveness of sins, the resurrection of the body, and the life everlasting. Amen.

Appendix A: In Case You Want to Know More

That First Kiss and Other Stories is one of five books in a series based on the principal beliefs of the Catholic faith. You may have noticed the italicized phrase at the end of each story. This phrase, which may be familiar to you, points to the particular topic highlighted in the story.

The first story of this book, "That First Kiss," has a concluding sentence that reads, "Let us profess our faith." These words—or similar ones—are said at the weekend Mass to invite the gathered community to proclaim its faith by reciting the creed. Several different Christian creeds have developed in the history of the church. The particular one used with the stories in this book is the Apostles' Creed.

Each story in this book is a mirror for understanding more deeply a particular aspect of the Apostles' Creed. If you want to know more about the Christian beliefs embodied in the stories, you can consult the following table. In this table, four sections appear for each story except the introductory story:

1. the creedal statement that the story is related to

2. the faith concept that the story illustrates
3. a relevant citation from the *Catechism of the Catholic Church*
4. a notation of paragraphs from the *Catechism* that provide background on the faith concept

"That First Kiss"

This story introduces the book. It also introduces the Good News of Jesus' message, Scripture and Tradition, and the Apostles' Creed as a summary of Christian belief.

"When You Care Enough to Give the Very Best"

1. "I believe in God . . ."
2. the Trinity, one God in three persons
3. "The mystery of the Most Holy Trinity is the central mystery of Christian faith and life" *(Catechism,* number 234).
4. *Catechism,* numbers 232 to 260

"The Best of Both Worlds"

1. ". . . the Father almighty . . ."
2. God as both Father and Mother
3. "God's parental tenderness can also be expressed by the image of motherhood, which emphasizes God's immanence, the intimacy between Creator and creature" *(Catechism,* number 239).
4. *Catechism,* numbers 238 to 242

"So, Big Deal!"
1. ". . . creator of heaven and earth."
2. creation and stewardship
3. "Nothing exists that does not owe its existence to God the Creator" (*Catechism*, number 338).
4. *Catechism*, numbers 337 to 349

"Seeing Double"
1. "I believe in Jesus Christ, his only Son, our Lord."
2. the Incarnation, Jesus as one person with two natures
3. "Jesus means in Hebrew: 'God saves'" (*Catechism*, number 430).
4. *Catechism*, numbers 430 to 451

"Waiting and Listening"
1. "He was conceived by the power of the Holy Spirit and born of the Virgin Mary."
2. the faith of Mary, the mother of Jesus
3. "Mary's role in the Church is inseparable from her union with Christ" (*Catechism*, number 964).
4. *Catechism*, numbers 487 to 507, and 963 to 972

"A New Way to Live and Die"
1. "He suffered under Pontius Pilate, was crucified, died, and was buried."
2. salvation, being saved by Jesus

3. "Jesus is the new Adam who remained faithful" (*Catechism,* number 539).
4. *Catechism,* numbers 571 to 628

"Back from the Dead"
1. "He descended into hell. On the third day he rose again."
2. resurrection, life after death
3. "Encounters with the risen Christ characterize the Christian hope of resurrection" (*Catechism,* number 995).
4. *Catechism,* numbers 638 to 655, and 992 to 1014

"The Light at the End of the Tunnel"
1. "He ascended into heaven and is seated at the right hand of the Father. He will come again to judge the living and the dead."
2. judgment, being judged by God
3. "The Last Judgment will reveal even to its furthest consequences the good each person has done or failed to do" (*Catechism,* number 1039).
4. *Catechism,* numbers 668 to 679, and 1038 to 1041

"Enjoying the Differences"
1. "I believe in the Holy Spirit . . ."
2. the Holy Spirit
3. "'The term "Spirit" translates the Hebrew word *ruah,* which, in its primary sense,

means breath, air, wind'" (*Catechism*, number 691).
4. *Catechism*, numbers 683 to 741

"A Glorious Night for an Eclipse"
1. ". . . the holy catholic Church . . ."
2. church, the people of God
3. "The Church is like the moon, all its light reflected from the sun" (*Catechism*, number 748).
4. *Catechism*, numbers 748 to 865

"My Own Special Saints in Heaven"
1. ". . . the communion of saints . . ."
2. the community of all believers
3. "'We believe in the communion of all the faithful of Christ, those who are pilgrims on earth, the dead who are being purified, and the blessed in heaven, all together forming one Church'" (*Catechism*, number 962).
4. *Catechism*, numbers 946 to 959

"A Little Bit of Heaven"
1. ". . . the forgiveness of sins, the resurrection of the body, and the life everlasting. Amen."
2. eternity, heaven
3. "God will then be 'all in all' in eternal life" (*Catechism*, number 1050).
4. *Catechism*, numbers 1020 to 1050

Appendix B: Series Chart

The stories in the books of this series were written to reflect the structure of the *Catechism of the Catholic Church.* Each book corresponds to a major section of the *Catechism,* and the stories in it correspond to some—not all—of the articles in that section. The following chart gives an overview of this connection. This chart can help youth ministry leaders, teachers, and catechists identify stories that relate to a particular topic or topics.

That First Kiss and Other Stories

This book is connected to part 1, "The Profession of Faith," of the *Catechism.* The individual stories in it correspond to sections of the Apostles' Creed. The following table identifies the faith theme explored by each story:

Story Title	*Faith Theme*
"That First Kiss"	Introduction
"When You Care Enough to Give the Very Best"	Trinity
"The Best of Both Worlds"	Image of God

"So, Big Deal!"	Creation and stewardship
"Seeing Double"	Incarnation
"Waiting and Listening"	Mary, mother of God
"A New Way to Live and Die"	Salvation
"Back from the Dead"	Resurrection
"The Light at the End of the Tunnel"	Last judgment
"Enjoying the Differences"	Holy Spirit
"A Glorious Night for an Eclipse"	Church, people of God
"My Own Special Saints in Heaven"	Communion of saints
"A Little Bit of Heaven"	Eternity, heaven

My Wish List and Other Stories

This book is connected to part 2, "The Celebration of the Christian Mystery," of the *Catechism.* The individual stories in it correspond to the seven sacraments. The following table identifies the sacrament explored by each story:

Story Title	*Sacrament*
"My Wish List"	Introduction

"College Jitters"	Baptism
"All That Matters"	Confirmation
"In Memory of Jesus"	Eucharist
"Do We Need Gas?"	Reconciliation
"Seeing Stars"	Anointing of the sick
"The Best Vocation in the World"	Holy orders
"Why Get Married?"	Marriage

Better than Natural and Other Stories

This book is connected to part 3, "Life in Christ," of the *Catechism*. The individual stories in it correspond to the formation of conscience and to the human and theological virtues. The following table identifies the virtue explored by each story:

Story Title	Virtue
"Better than Natural"	Introduction
"To Cheat or Not to Cheat"	Conscience formation
"Pink Flowers Instead of Yellow"	Prudence
"People Who Are Not Like Us"	Justice

"This Is Unreal"	Fortitude (courage)
"The Big College Weekend"	Temperance
"Gee, Joy, I Don't Think So"	Faith
"Paints and Flowers"	Hope
"The Best Medicine"	Love (charity)

Straight from the Heart and Other Stories

This book is also connected to part 3, "Life in Christ," of the *Catechism*. The individual stories in it correspond to the Ten Commandments. The following table identifies the moral teaching explored by each story:

Story Title	*Moral Teaching*
"Straight from the Heart"	Introduction
"Taking a Cookie Break"	Hold God as number one.
"Ice Cream, TV, and Baby-Sitting"	Respect God's name.
"The Guy in the Tie"	Value sacred time and space.
"A Real Man"	Respect your parents.

"It's Wrong No Matter Who Does It"	Hold all human life sacred.
"Chris and Lee in Action"	Be faithful in marriage.
"More Money Than God"	Respect the possessions of others.
"Pushing the Limits of Honesty"	Be truthful.
"Two Opposite Conversations"	Be grateful and detached from possessions.

Meeting Frankenstein and Other Stories

This book is connected to part 4, "Christian Prayer," of the *Catechism*. The individual stories in it correspond to sections of the Lord's Prayer and to different types of prayer. The following table identifies the type of prayer explored by each story:

Story Title	*Type of Prayer*
"Meeting Frankenstein"	Introduction
"Oh, My God!"	Praise
"I Want to Tell You How Great I Think You Are"	Adoration and blessing
"Thank God!"	Thanksgiving

"Why Didn't You Answer My Prayers?"	Petition
"Playing with Fire"	Sorrow
"Asking for Too Much"	Intercession
"Sitting on Life's Park Bench"	Meditation
"Empty Your Head and Let God Fill It"	Contemplation

Acknowledgments *(continued)*

The scriptural passage in the dedication to this book is quoted from the New American Bible, giant print edition. Copyright © 1976 by Catholic Publishers, a division of Thomas Nelson. All rights reserved.

The scriptural passage described as adapted on pages 42–43 is freely paraphrased and is not to be used or understood as an official translation of the Bible.

The scriptural passages on pages 52 and 61 are quoted from 1 Corinthians 15:17 and Leviticus 19:18 in the New Revised Standard Version of the Bible. Copyright © 1989 by the Division of Christian Education of the National Council of the Churches of Christ in the United States of America. All rights reserved.

The words of the Apostles' Creed in the concluding statements for the stories and in appendix A are from the Catechism of the Catholic Church, by the Libreria Editrice Vaticana, translated by the United States Catholic Conference (USCC) (Washington, DC: USCC, 1994), pages 49–50. English translation copyright © 1994 by the USCC—Libreria Editrice Vaticana. The relevant citations in appendix A are also from this source, numbers 234, 239, 338, 430, 964, 539, 995, 1039, 691, 748, 962, and 1050, as noted.

The words of Saint Augustine on page 80 are paraphrased from *The Confessions of St. Augustine,* translated by F. J. Sheed (New York: Sheed and Ward, 1943), page 3. Copyright © 1943 by Sheed and Ward.

Titles in the Series

That First Kiss and Other Stories
My Wish List and Other Stories
Better than Natural and Other Stories
Straight from the Heart and Other Stories
Meeting Frankenstein and Other Stories

Order these titles from your local religious bookstore, or from us in one of these ways:

- Write to us at this address:
  Saint Mary's Press
  702 Terrace Heights
  Winona MN 55987-1320
- Call us at 800-533-8095.
- Look us up on the Internet at
  www.smp.org.